Dig Up Your Roots and
Find Your Branches

Dig Up Your Roots and Find Your Branches

A Child's Guide to Genealogy

Susan H. Hubbs

Writer's Showcase
presented by *Writer's Digest*
San Jose New York Lincoln Shanghai

Dig Up Your Roots and Find Your Branches
A Child's Guide to Genealogy

Writer's Showcase
presented by *Writer's Digest*
an imprint of iUniverse.com, Inc.

For information address:
iUniverse.com, Inc.
620 North 48th Street, Suite 201
Lincoln, NE 68504-3467
www.iuniverse.com

ISBN: 0-595-13162-X

Printed in the United States of America

Dedicated to Christopher and Elizabeth, whose youthful editing and wisdom provided insight well beyond their years. I am so grateful for their steadfast and loving encouragement.

Contents

Preface

Step Back In Time

Take a big step back in time;
Climb up your family tree.
Begin the search for kinship ties;
Discover your ancestry!

Dig up your roots and find those branches
Of ancestors long ago.
A relative could be Jesse James…
You may not want to know!

It could be that your family comes from
Dukes or queens or kings.
Or you may find a relative
Who loved to dance and sing!

You could learn of an ancestor
Who fought in the Civil War.
He may have been a general…
A leader to the core.

So many stories can be learned
About your family.
Begin a journey into your past.
You'll love genealogy!

Susan H. Hubbs

Introduction

Genealogy—What Is It?

Have you ever wanted to travel in a time machine? Do you enjoy puzzles and mysteries? Do you think you'd make an awesome detective? Then get ready to turn the pages of this book and discover all of the fun and excitement that **genealogy** has to offer!

Genealogy is the history of you and your family. It is sometimes called a family tree. Studying the history of your family will take you back in time, as far as you want to go! Who knows? Maybe you are a **descendant** of Abraham Lincoln, a European king, or even an outlaw like Jesse James. Follow the easy steps in this book and you may find a famous person hiding behind the branches in *your* family tree!

Before you begin, there are special parts of this book that will help you learn about genealogy. If you stumble across a word you don't understand, it may be printed in **bold** letters. You can look up any word that is printed in **bold** letters in the "Genealogy Dictionary" at the back of this book!

Throughout the book, you will come across "Family Tree Facts". These facts are important bits of information that you should always keep in mind while working on your family history. You will recognize the "Family Tree Facts" because of the nearby tree that looks like this:

You will also find helpful charts, a family tree, a supply checklist, puzzles and much more fun inside the pages of *"Dig Up Your Roots and Find Your Branches!"*

Now that you understand a little bit about this book, you are ready to begin a journey into the past…*your* past. So hold on to your trunk and let's shake loose those ancestors!

Chapter 1

Stock Up Your Genealogical Toolbox

Have you ever heard the old saying, "I am not my brother's keeper"? Well throw that thought right out the window, because as a **genealogist**, you *are* the keeper of all of your family records!

SUPPLIES

Since you will be collecting a lot of information, you must be organized. One important way to get organized is to have the correct supplies. All you really need to begin is a pencil and paper, but there are a few other items that, although not necessary, will help keep your **data** neat and in order. They are:

- **Three Notebooks (three-ring binder style):** You will need one "three-ring binder" for your father's side of the family, one for your mother's side of the family, and a third notebook to hold assorted maps, charts, and notes.

- **Tabbed notebook dividers:** You will want to divide your notebooks into different sections as you gather more and more data!

- **Highlighting marker:** To highlight important information that can be noticed quickly.

- **Hole puncher:** Will come in handy for inserting charts inside your notebooks.

- **Blank pedigree charts:** A "ready-to-use" family tree chart can be found inside this book! (See Chapter 3) Or you can create your own charts!

- **Magnifying glass:** You may need to examine old and faded documents.

- **Floppy disks:** Necessary if you plan to use a computer and want to safely store your data.

- **Acid-free plastic sheet protectors:** For protecting photographs and documents from dirt and fingerprints.

- **Acid-free paper:** This is suggested for all genealogical keepsakes.

- **Tote bag:** Helpful for trips to the library!

I HAVE MY SUPPLIES...NOW WHAT?

When you have collected your supplies, you need to make a plan to keep your records in order. One way to do this is to begin a filing system. A filing system is simply a way to keep your valuable **data** from getting lost or misplaced!

Begin by getting out two of your notebooks. One notebook will be for your father's family. Label the outside of this notebook with your father's **surname**, or last name. All of the information you collect on your father's family should be placed inside this notebook.

Use the second notebook for your mother's family. Label this notebook with your mother's **maiden** surname. All of the information you collect on your mother's family should be placed inside this notebook. To help you understand the term **maiden name**, here's an example:

When your mother was born, pretend her name was Jane Elizabeth Jones. This is called her maiden name. When she married Sam Smith her name changed to Jane Jones Smith. For your family tree records, you should list her with the JONES family as Jane Elizabeth Jones because that is her maiden name, the name she was born with. There will be another place where you can write the name of her husband.

"Family Tree Fact"

*In genealogy, when you record information about a woman, always use her maiden name, **not** her last name after she married.*

After you have labeled your two notebooks, get out several of your tabbed dividers. Label one of the dividers with your father's surname and put it into his family notebook. Label another divider with your mother's surname and insert it into her family notebook.

Now you are ready to learn one of the most important ways to be a successful genealogist!

Chapter 2

Document Your Sources!
Document Your Sources!
Document Your Sources!

Is something wrong with the printer? Do you need a new pair of eye-glasses? NO! This chapter is so important that it can't be said enough! DOCUMENT YOUR SOURCES!!!

What exactly does that mean? Simply put, it means this: Make a note about where you get each piece of information. For example, if Aunt Betsy told you that her grandfather, John Wilson, was born in 1900, then you should write down beside John Wilson's birth date that Betsy Wilson gave you that information. If you found his birth place on a birth certificate, make a note of that, too. If you discovered the date of his death by looking at a gravestone, write it down!

You could make your notes like this:

John Mark Wilson
born: 1900 (source: Betsy Wilson)
birthplace: Pittsburgh, PA (source: John Mark Wilson's birth certificate)
died: 5 August, 1965 (source: gravestone at Bay Cemetery, Green City, Payne Co., SD)

Why is it so important to document your sources? First, there will be many times when you might need to go back and look at something again. In five years, you will not be able to remember which book you read or who told you the information. Writing down the source will save you a lot of time and frustration.

Also, once you have collected a lot of data, other researchers may ask you to share what you know. When you share your family tree with someone, they will want to know that the data you are sharing is correct! No one wants to put anything into their database that isn't true, so if you can provide sources, anyone can easily verify what you have generously shared!

Likewise, if you receive family history from someone else, make sure that you check out their sources before entering the information into your database. Make a note of the name and address of the person who gave you the new data.

"Family Tree Fact"

Always make a note about where you obtained each fact.
This is called "documenting your sources".

DATES AND LOCATIONS

It is especially important to know the correct way to write down dates and locations. Most genealogy researchers who are serious about their work write down dates and locations in the same way as professional genealogists. This is helpful when you share your data with others, or when you are lucky enough to receive data from someone else! The correct way to write a date is to first put the number date, then the month, then the year, like this:

05 August, 1965

Do *not* write the date with slashed or dashes like this:

8/5/65 or 8-5-65

Using slashes or dashes could mean lots of different dates. In some countries the date 3-5-65 would mean the third month, fifth day, which would be March 5th. In other countries the same numbers would mean the third day of the fifth month, which would be May 3rd!

And take a look at the year. Can you see how this could be 1765, 1865, or 1965? Remember that your **ancestors** will one day be looking at the work you are doing. Don't make them guess!

"Family Tree Fact"

Always write the date in its correct form.
(Correct example: 05 June, 1847)

Just like there are rules for writing dates, there are certain ways that you should write down locations. Always write the city or **township** first, then the county, then the state, then the country. Here are two examples:

Orlando, Orange Co., FL, USA

Paradise Twp., York, PA, USA

Any genealogist who reads this will know that in the first example, I am writing about the city of Orlando, located in Orange County, in the state of Florida, in the United States of America. The second example refers to Paradise Township, located in York County, Pennsylvania, in the United States.

Now take out a piece of paper and try to write your birth date as a genealogist would write it. Then, remembering what you just learned, practice writing down where you live, in a way that another researcher would understand. Next, try writing where you were born. Do you need help with state abbreviations? There is a helpful chart in the back of this book!

SURNAMES

You will soon discover that it is much easier to look over a page of information and find what you are searching for when it is written in all capital letters. Take a look at the following sentences:

Mary Jane Smith lived in New York.

Mary Jane SMITH lived in New York.

If you are researching the name "Smith", which sentence reaches out and grabs your attention? The sentence with capital letters, of course!

KEEP IT NEAT!

No, I'm not fussing about your bedroom. I'm talking about your handwriting! If you have access to a computer, word processor, or a typewriter, it's best to use them. If you don't own one of these machines, do not fear! Some of the world's best genealogists use good, old-fashioned handwriting! Just remember…no cursive writing! Use only your very best printing so that in years to come, no one will need a magnifying glass to understand what you've written!

BOOK SOURCES

Let's say you have found some important information in the book, *Smith Family History*. There is a proper way to document this source. You should list the name of the book, the author, the publisher, and the publication date. Also include the place where you found the book (library, Aunt Betsy's house, etc.) and the page number(s).

For example, if you found William Smith's birth place in the book, *Smith Family History*, you might document it in your records like this:

William Jonathan SMITH

born: 04 June, 1751

place of birth: Hopewell Twp., Lancaster Co., PA, USA

(source: **Smith Family History**, John A. Smith, Treehouse Publishers, 1975, Lancaster County Public Library, pg., 56.)

Never forget the golden rule of genealogy: DOCUMENT YOUR SOURCES!!!

MAKE COPIES AND KEEP GOOD RECORDS!

Whenever you are lucky enough to find important family papers, you may not be able to keep the original document. In that case, simply make copies. There is no better source to have than the actual document, but a good, clear copy is the next best thing! If you have copies of birth certificates, death certificates, or marriage licenses, insert them inside clear, plastic, acid-free sheet protectors. Place these into the appropriate family notebook.

Keep a record of every scrap of information…especially when the data is conflicting. For instance, if the date in your great-grandfather's **obituary** says something different than what your grandmother told you, make a note of both dates for future refer-ence. You may one day find that they are both wrong!

Now that you have your supplies in order and you know the importance of keeping track of your sources, you are ready to begin the exciting journey into your past!

Chapter 3

Shake the Ancestors From Your Tree!

In order to begin your journey back in time, you must first learn all that you can about the present. Think about this question:

Who is the one person in your family that you know best?

The answer is *you*, of course! All family researchers will tell you that the place to begin the search for your roots is with yourself!

INDIVIDUAL WORKSHEETS

Let's start by creating an "individual worksheet" about yourself. Use the examples found at the end of this chapter to design your own worksheets. Your Individual Worksheet should include the following:

- **Full name** (first, middle, and last)
- **Nicknames** (if any)
- **Birth date** (remember to use the correct format!)
- **Birth place** (can you make a copy of the birth certificate?)
- **Father's full name**

- **Mother's full name** (remember that your mother probably had a different surname before she was married. It's called her maiden name.)
- **Baptism/christening date and place**
- **Hobbies, schools, awards, special activities, occupation**

After completing a worksheet about yourself, move on to your parents. Fill out an individual worksheet for your mother and one for your father. Ask them for the same information you wrote down about yourself, but add the following:

- **Marriage date and place** (Ask if you can make a copy of the marriage certificate. Keep it in a plastic, acid-free sheet protector in your father's family three-ring binder notebook.)
- **Children's full names and birth information**

Congratulations! You have completed the first step in researching your family tree. You have now traced back one **generation**! Did you remember to document your sources? If the answer is yes, then you are ready to go back *two* generations. Can you guess whose "individual worksheets" you need to complete next? If you said your grandparents, you're exactly right!

Your mother and father may be able to help you with a lot of data on your grandparents, especially if they are no longer living. But, if possible, it's always a good idea to talk to your grandparents yourself. You never know what kind of juicy stories you might uncover in the conversation!

"JUST THE FACTS MA'AM"— SECRETS TO A GOOD INTERVIEW

So you'd like to interview a family member? Great idea! You'll be surprised at how much information you can get from an interview. Just like a good reporter, you need to remember six questions that will get you the answers you are searching for. Who, What, Where, When, Why and How?

For example:

- **Who** are your brothers and sister?
- **What** are some of your fondest memories?
- **Where** did you go to school?
- **When** did you get married?
- **Why** did you become a teacher?
- **How** did you meet grandma?

When asking your relatives for information, don't concentrate only on the dates. A family file full of numbers can get very dull! You definitely *need* dates for your research, but consider using the six reporter questions to dig a little deeper. Other questions you may want to use in your interviews are:

- Where did you grow up?
- Did you live in one house or did you move around?
- Describe your house.

- Tell me about your schools.

- Who was your favorite teacher and why?

- What is your highest level of education?

- Did you serve in the military? Ask for details.

- Were your parents born in another state? In another country?

- Describe your **occupation**. Did you have more than one job?

Can you see how these questions will make your family history come alive? Instead of being just a name and a few boring dates, your family member is taking the shape of an interesting and unique person!

"Family Tree Fact"

Be sure not to miss a thing—use a tape recorder in your interviews.
In years to come, the tape will be a family treasure!
(Of course, first get permission from the person you are interviewing.)

WRITE LETTERS!

You might have relatives that you'd like to personally interview, but if they live very far away, it won't be easy to jump on your bike and ride over for a face-to-face chat! So how do you get the scoop on these distant family members? By writing a good old-fashioned letter!

Begin by writing a simple note. Explain about your new hobby and the type of information you are looking for. You can use what you have learned about conducting a good interview and put it on paper!

Remember the six questions a reporter always uses? Who, What, Where, When, Why and How. In your letter you could also include a copy of an "individual worksheet" for them to fill out and return to you. You'll get a faster response if you include a self-addressed, stamped envelope!

CLEAN OUT THOSE COBWEBS!

After your letters are in the mail, and you have interviewed all of your family members, it's time to do some house cleaning. WHAT!!! HOUSE CLEANING?!!! What does house cleaning have to do with your family history? Not much, if you're thinking about vacuuming, ironing and washing dishes. But you may be surprised to know that by simply dusting off a few cobwebs and searching in rarely visited places, you could discover a wealth of family history!

Your attic or basement is a great place to start. Ask an adult relative to go with you. They can be a big help by pointing you in the right direction. After you've "cleaned up" in those places, do you have a room in the house that's full of junk drawers? It could be a gold mine of historical data just waiting to be found!

By now I'm sure you're wondering, "What exactly am I looking for?"

One household book that genealogists find very helpful is the family Bible. If your family has a Bible that has been passed down from generation to generation, it is sure to be full of valuable names and dates. Why? Because before the 1900's, birth certificates and marriage licenses were not required. And since life in those times usually revolved around family and church, the family Bible was a natural place to keep important facts.

Take a look at the list on the next page to discover many other places you can find facts about your family!

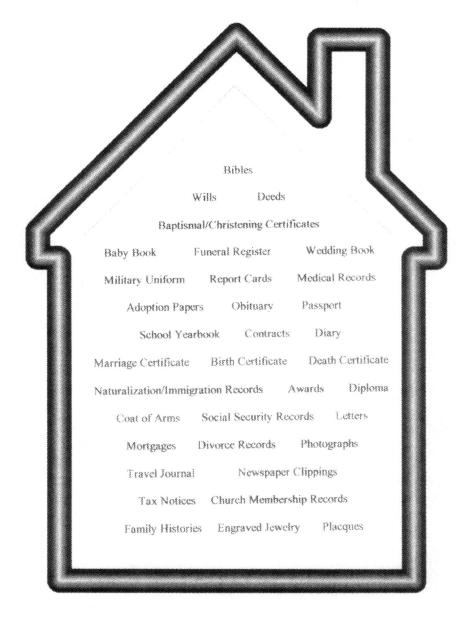

Bibles

Wills   Deeds

Baptismal/Christening Certificates

Baby Book   Funeral Register   Wedding Book

Military Uniform   Report Cards   Medical Records

Adoption Papers   Obituary   Passport

School Yearbook   Contracts   Diary

Marriage Certificate   Birth Certificate   Death Certificate

Naturalization/Immigration Records   Awards   Diploma

Coat of Arms   Social Security Records   Letters

Mortgages   Divorce Records   Photographs

Travel Journal   Newspaper Clippings

Tax Notices   Church Membership Records

Family Histories   Engraved Jewelry   Placques

FAMILY GROUP SHEETS

Every respectable genealogist knows the value of keeping family group sheets. Family group sheets are a report about each family. Each marriage will have its own separate family group sheet. For example, if one man was married three times, then he will have three different family group sheets.

Using the family group sheets found at the end of this chapter, make up a family group sheet for your family. Your family group sheet will have your father's name and his data. Below your father's information, you will fill in data on your mother. Underneath your parents is where you write down the facts about their children, you and your siblings.

Next, make a family group sheet on your **paternal grandparents.** (Your paternal grandparents are the parents of your father.) After that is completed, make a family group sheet on your **maternal grandparents.** (Your maternal grandparents are the parents of your mother.) You will need to make a family group sheet for each and every marriage you discover in your family history. Family group sheets should be kept in that family's three-ring binder notebook.

PEDIGREE CHARTS

A **pedigree chart** is what most people think of when they hear the term "family tree." It is a diagram that shows you and all of the generations before you. Your goal as a genealogist is to find your long-lost **ancestors** by researching your pedigree line as far back as you are able to go!

"Family Tree Fact"

A pedigree chart shows only your direct line of ancestors.
It does not include brothers, sisters, aunts or uncles.

Find the blank **pedigree chart** located at the end of this chapter. It looks like a tree with many empty boxes inside the tree. Enlarge it and make a few copies of the chart, or bring out the artist within you and design your own family tree!

Each box should contain a full name, birth date and death date. Start by putting your name and birth date inside the box labeled "1". Next, follow the line from your box up to the box labeled "2". Put your father's data inside this box. Follow the line from your box up to the box labeled "3". This is where your mother's name and dates should be written.

Next, follow the lines from your father's box to box "4" and box "5". Can you guess who goes in these boxes? If you said your **paternal grandparents**, you are right! Your father's father goes into box "4", and your father's mother goes into box "5". Now do the same with your mother's parents. You can continue to create your family pedigree, going back as far as your information will let you! Do you see how the different **generations** branch out, just like a living tree?

Keep your **pedigree chart** inside your third three-ring binder. This will be the notebook you take along with you when you leave home to do research. To continue your ancestral search, you will be traveling to churches, the library, and maybe even a cemetery or two! So grab your walking shoes and let's go!

INDIVIDUAL WORKSHEET

NAME:_____

     First   *Middle*   *(Maiden)*   *Last*

BIRTH DATE:_____

               Date/Month/Year

BIRTHPLACE:_____

               City/County/State

FATHER:_____

     First   *Middle*   *Last*   *(Jr, Sr)*

FATHER'S BIRTH DATE:_____

               Date/Month/Year

FATHER'S BIRTHPLACE_____

               City/County/State

FATHER'S DATE OF DEATH:_____

FATHER'S PLACE OF BURIAL_____

LAST KNOWN RESIDENCE:_____

MOTHER:_____

     First   *Middle*   *Maiden*   *Last*

MOTHER'S BIRTH DATE:_____

Date/Month/Year

MOTHER'S BIRTHPLACE_____

City/County/State

MOTHER'S DATE OF DEATH:_____

MOTHER'S PLACE OF BURIAL_____

LAST KNOWN RESIDENCE:_____

MATERNAL GRANDFATHER:_____

DATE OF BIRTH_____ BIRTH PLACE_____

DATE OF DEATH_____

PLACE OF BURIAL_____

MATERNAL GRANDMOTHER:_____

DATE OF BIRTH_____ BIRTH PLACE_____

DATE OF DEATH_____

PLACE OF BURIAL_____

PATERNAL GRANDFATHER:_____

DATE OF BIRTH_____ BIRTH PLACE_____

DATE OF DEATH_____

PLACE OF BURIAL_____

PATERNAL GRANDMOTHER:_____

DATE OF BIRTH_____ BIRTH PLACE_____

DATE OF DEATH_____

PLACE OF BURIAL_____

SPOUSE:_____

    First   *Middle*   *Maiden*   *Last*

SPOUSE DATE OF BIRTH:_____

SPOUSE BIRTH PLACE:_____

SPOUSE DATE OF DEATH:_____

PLACE OF BURIAL:_____

CHILD #1:_____
      First   *Middle*   *Last*

DATE OF BIRTH:_____

BIRTH PLACE:_____

CHILD #2_____
      First   *Middle*   *Last*

DATE OF BIRTH:_____

BIRTH PLACE:_____

CHILD #3:_____
      First   *Middle*   *Last*
DATE OF BIRTH:_____

BIRTH PLACE:_____

CHILD #4_____
       First   *Middle*   *Last*

DATE OF BIRTH:_____

BIRTH PLACE:_____

CHILD #5_____
       First   *Middle*   *Last*

DATE OF BIRTH:_____

BIRTH PLACE:_____

SIBLING #1:_____
       First   *Middle*   *Last*

DATE OF BIRTH:_____ SPOUSE:_____
SIBLING #2:_____
       First   *Middle*   *Last*

DATE OF BIRTH:_____ SPOUSE:_____

SIBLING #3:_____

      First   *Middle*   *Last*

DATE OF BIRTH:_____ SPOUSE:_____

SIBLING #4:_____

      First   *Middle*   *Last*

DATE OF BIRTH:_____ SPOUSE:_____

SIBLING #5:_____

      First   *Middle*   *Last*

DATE OF BIRTH:_____ SPOUSE:_____

SIBLING #6:_____

      First   *Middle*   *Last*

DATE OF BIRTH:_____SPOUSE:_____

SIBLING #7:_____

      First   *Middle*   *Last*

DATE OF BIRTH:_____ SPOUSE:_____

Family Group Sheet

Husband:

    Birth Date:

    Birth Place:

    Death Date:

    Death Place:

    Burial Date:

    Burial Place:

    Married:

    Marriage Date:

    Marriage Place:

    Father:

    Mother:

Wife:

    Birth Date:

    Birth Place:

    Death Date:

    Death Place:

    Burial Date:

    Burial Place:

    Father:

    Mother:

Children:

1. Name:
   Birth Date:
   Birth Place:
   Death Date:
   Death Place:
   Burial Date:
   Burial Place:
   Married:
   Marriage Date:

2. Name:
   Birth Date:
   Birth Place:
   Death Date:
   Death Place:
   Burial Date:
   Burial Place:
   Married:
   Marriage Date:

3. Name:
   Birth Date:
   Birth Place:
   Death Date:
   Death Place:

Burial Date:
Burial Place:
Married:
Marriage Date:

4. Name:
Birth Date:
Birth Place:
Death Date:
Death Place:
Burial Date:
Burial Place:
Married:
Marriage Date:

5. Name:
Birth Date:
Birth Place:
Death Date:
Death Place:
Burial Date:
Burial Place:
Married:
Marriage Date:

Chapter 4

Where In the World Are Your Forefathers?

"Where in the world are your **forefathers**?" The answer is: They could be *anywhere*. And when no one in your family can answer your questions, you must search elsewhere for the keys to unlock your past. Tracking down this missing information can be easy, *if* you know how to use the many resources that are available to you. This chapter will teach you what those resources are and how to use them!

THE LIBRARY: A FAMILY FRIEND

The library is a place, full of wisdom, knowledge, and of course, books. But you may not know that many libraries, especially the main branches in large cities, have a special section devoted entirely to genealogy! In the genealogy section of the library, you may find books on specific surnames, county history, ship passenger lists, military records, census records, and so much more!

You should know, however, that the genealogy section is very different from the rest of the library. They have different rules about what you may, and may not check out. Since many of the documents are old and irreplaceable, most of the items are not allowed to be removed from the library. Make sure you have a pencil and plenty of paper to make notes of any interesting facts you may stumble across. Remember to document your sources!

Most genealogy sections have a copy machine available. For a small fee (usually 10-25 cents per page) you can make a copy of your genealogical find. So start saving some of that allowance money for your trips to the library!

WHAT IS THE CENSUS? WHY DO I NEED IT?

The genealogy section of your library will have a special area which holds the **census** records.

The census is an official count of the number of people living in a certain area. The United States began performing the census in 1790, and continues to collect this information every ten years. When you look back at old census records, you may find names of all family members, their ages and where they were born. Sometimes only the head of household, usually the father or a **widow**, will be listed.

In the library, census data is organized on **microfilm** or **microfiche**, usually in large drawers, according to the year and the state. After you have located the year and state you are interested in, you must narrow your search down to the county. Once you have found the county, state, and year you need, take the microfilm box out of the drawer and ask the librarian to teach you how to use the microfilm machine. Pay attention to this lesson, because as a genealogist, you will spend many hours at this piece of equipment!

Once you are able to operate the microfilm, you can begin searching for the surname of the person you are seeking. Names are found at the far left-hand side of the census document. Beside each name, you will see different information. Some census reports will have lots of data, and others will have very little.

On microfilm, many times the counties are divided into towns, so you may be able to go directly to the section of microfilm where the census of the town you need is located. If you do not know the town, you can search the entire film, or look in the **census index**. The census index is a series of books usually located near the census microfilm. Like the microfilm, the books are divided into years and states. In the census index, you can select a year and a state, then look up a person's name and find out which page on the microfilm that person can be found! This will save you lots of time at the microfilm machine!

Once you have located your relative in the microfilm census records, you need to document your findings. Take out a piece of paper and write down everything you see on the census document: year, state and county, parish, town, district or city, microfilm number, names of your ancestors, age, and any other vital information contained in the census. You may want to use ready-made charts which can be found on the Internet and printed out for easy use! Go to:

http://www.CyndisList.com/census.htm#Forms/

These charts are perfect for copying and keeping track of census findings!

If you uncover a census document that is especially important to you, make a copy. Many microfilm machines allow you to make copies, for a price, usually around fifty cents.

GET YOUR NEWSPAPER & READ ALL ABOUT IT!

Wouldn't it be great to find articles written about your ancestors in past copies of "The Daily News" or "The Anytown Gazette"? Since most libraries keep copies of old newspapers on microfilm or microfiche, you may be able to uncover some surprises lurking among the sheets of old newspapers!

The section of a newspaper that is most useful to a genealogist is the **obituary** section. Here's why:

Suppose you know where an ancestor was living and the date of their death. Take a look in the local newspaper one or two days *after* the death date. If you can located the obituary, many times the notice will list parents, **spouse**, children, and life long activities. This could be information you have been searching for!

"Family Tree Fact"

If the library doesn't have the newspaper you need,
go directly to the newspaper office.
They will have copies of all back issues.

WHERE ELSE CAN I SEARCH?

The library is not the only place to find records on your family. Some other locations you can do research include: **archives**, court houses, churches and the Social Security office.

The archives is a place where many old private and public records are kept and preserved. Like the library, you may not leave the building with any books or documents. Many times the archives and the library have the same data, but since this is not always the case, you should make a visit to the local archives if one is nearby.

Inside county court houses, you can find deeds, marriage records, divorce records, tax lists and wills. Since this information is public record, that means anyone can ask to see these documents. Deeds will show who owned a certain piece of land, when they owned it, and who sold it to them. Marriage and divorce records can help you with names and dates. Tax lists can help determine where a relative lived and what kind of property they owned. Wills can help with death dates and will sometimes list certain family members.

If you know the church that your forefathers attended, there may be records on file in the church on confirmations, communions, meeting minutes, baptismal/christening records, membership records, plus data on births, deaths and marriages.

Since the 1930's, everyone who has worked at a job must have a social security number. If you have the social security number of any **deceased** relatives, you can write to the Social Security office and request the records of that person. You will be able to find out their date of birth and when they died. You should be aware that the Social Security Administration charges fees for certain services.

LDS FAMILY HISTORY CENTERS

Latter-Day Saints Family History Centers, commonly called LDS History Centers, are some of the greatest sources of information to genealogists. The centers are located all over the world, and although they are privately owned and most are located in the meetinghouses of the Church of Jesus Christ of Latter-Day Saints, anyone may use the centers. The volunteers who work at the centers are very friendly and knowledgeable. They are not there to discuss religion with you. The volunteers are there to assist you with your family history.

The LDS History Centers have many computer files you are free to explore. One of these files is a collection of family histories which has been donated by many different researchers. Be careful how you use this information because it could contain mistakes. As with any data you collect from someone else, always check and document your findings before placing it into your own database.

Another file found at the LDS Centers uses data taken from actual documents. This file contains birth dates and places, plus christenings and marriages of many people who lived between 1500 and 1900.

All of the LDS Centers are connected to the Family History Library in Salt Lake City, Utah. They have a huge microfilm collection, over two million rolls! This microfilm contains copies of original records which are of great value to family researchers. But you don't have to fly out to Utah to see these records. Copies of these films can be ordered through your local LDS History Center!

"Family Tree Fact"

To find the LDS Center closest to your home, call Family History Support at 1-800-346-6044.

CEMETERIES

Do visions of ghosts and goblins keep you out of cemeteries? Then it's time for you to bury those fears right now! Ask your parents to plan a trip during the day and visit the final resting places of some of your ancestors. You might want to take along a camera, white paper, and dark colored chalk. When you arrive at the grave sites of your relatives, don't be squeamish! Look upon this as another adventure for you, the detective!

Copy down all of the information from each gravestone. You might want to snap some pictures. On very old gravestones, you may have a difficult time reading the words. This is where the paper and chalk come in handy. You can make a **gravestone rubbing**. Simply hold the paper flat up against the stone and rub the chalk back and forth across the paper. The words on the gravestone will magically appear onto your paper!

A few words of advice about gravestone rubbings:

Some cemeteries require that you get permission before rubbing.

Make sure the stone is in good condition. You don't want to apply pressure and knock down a gravestone.

Be careful not to color onto the gravestone.

Pick up all of your trash. Leave the cemetery cleaner than you found it!

Remember! A nice rubbing is a unique work of art, as well as a genealogical document. Handle your rubbing with care!

"Family Tree Fact"

Professional "rubbers" use a special ball of wax to make beautiful rubbings that can be framed.
Find a book in the library if you are interested in learning more about gravestone rubbings.

Chapter 5

The Pen and the Pentium—
A Winning Combination!

Computers have quickly become important to people and businesses everywhere. Genealogists are no different, but floppy disks and the World Wide Web will never totally replace pen and paper in genealogical research. There will always be a need to keep precious, original records and documents, but if you have access to a home computer, by all means, *use it*! This chapter will reveal what family history researchers everywhere are discovering: the many ways that computers can bring your ancestors directly into your home!

INTERNET RULES AND TOOLS

The Internet is a system with thousands of networks and millions of computers working together to share information. It is often called the "information superhighway".

If your home computer allows you access to the Internet, you are in luck! The Internet will allow you to search all over the world for information about your ancestors. The first rule when using the Internet is to *always* get your parents permission before doing any kind of search. Better yet, turn this into a family activity and work together on the computer!

You may wonder why Internet safety is such a big deal. Here's why:

Since you don't personally know all of the people sitting at all of those computers, you must be careful about how much information you give out, and just as cautious about believing the information you take in. Surfing the Internet is like taking a trip to a faraway place. Just as you wouldn't make this kind of journey without a parent or responsible adult, you shouldn't travel around the Internet without a parent or trustworthy adult. Internet safety is the number one rule. Don't break it!

SEARCH ENGINES

One important Internet research tool is the "search engine." Search engines do exactly what you think they do. They search out and find web sites dealing with a subject that interests you. Web sites are pages that you can read while you are connected to the Internet. It's easy to find web sites about your family name using search engines.

How do you get to a search engine? Your home computer may be set up with a "search" button that will take you directly to a search engine. Or you can go to one of the addresses listed below:

- www.webcrawler.com
- www.excite.com
- www.lycos.com
- www.yahoo.com

- www.go.com
- www.mckinley.com
- www.metacrawler.com

These are only a few of the many available search engines, but this list will help you begin your computer search.

After choosing a search engine, type in its Internet address and you will be taken to the search page. On your screen you should see a blank box. In this box, type in one word, (or several words) which describe the information you are seeking. For example, you may want to search for sites about the SMITH family. You can type the word "Smith" in the box (without quotation marks!). You could also type in the words "Smith Family", or "Smith+family". Click on "search" and the search engine will return a list of all sites that matches those words! Next, simply choose a site from the list that interests you. Click on it and presto! You are there!

When you have finished exploring that web site, click your "back" button to return to your search list and pick out another one to try. Continue to do this until you feel there is nothing else to be found on this search engine. Then follow the same procedure with a new set of words or try a different search engine.

A few possible search engine word combinations to try are:

- Smith
- Smith family
- Smith family tree
- Smith family research
- Smith family genealogy
- Smith genealogy

- Smith family heritage
- Smith ancestry
- Smith heritage

Of course, you will want to use the surnames *you* are research-ing…not SMITH (unless that is your name!)

ELECTRONIC MAIL

Electronic mail, or e-mail, is an excellent way to use the computer to further your family research. E-mail allows you to write a message and then use the Internet to deliver that message. You can think of the Internet as being a superhuman mailman, delivering family his-tory data across the world almost instantly!

Before you correspond with a stranger, remember these Internet rules:

- **NEVER** use the Internet, including e-mail, without a parent's permission and guidance.
- **VERIFY** all data before accepting it as the truth.

It's also a great idea to print important e-mail messages and keep them in your three-ring binders. You may want to make a new index divider for each family notebook. Label the divider "e-mail" and keep all messages you receive in this section.

It's also smart to keep copies of these letters on a floppy disk. That gives you extra insurance just in case your paperwork gets lost or damaged. Label your disks "SMITH FAMILY E-MAIL", or something similar. Use a new disk for each different surname.

Always make back-up copies of all computer work. It's a super habit to get into, and will be helpful in every kind of computer creation, not just family research!

GENEALOGY SOFTWARE SECRETS

You will find that a wide choice of software is available for keeping family history records on your home computer. Computer programs are an excellent way to organize and keep track of your work. Most of these programs will print out beautiful family trees, perfect for sharing! Genealogy software costs from ten dollars up to eighty or more dollars, the average being thirty to sixty dollars. Baby-sitting or mowing the lawn might enable you to purchase one of these higher priced programs. But before you spend that hard earned cash, there are a few other options you should investigate!

First, many companies frequently offer rebates when you purchase their software. A rebate is an offer from the company that guarantees they will return a certain amount of money to you if you buy their product. By taking advantage of a rebate offer, you can save quite a few dollars. Many genealogy programs can even be obtained for free after sending in the manufacturer's rebate. Be on the lookout in newspaper ads for these terrific deals!

You can also take advantage of an Internet site, Kindred Konnections, where you can download a free genealogy program! Ask your parents if you can keep your family history on the computer. If they say yes, and you don't want to spend money or wait for a rebate offer to be announced, then take a look at Kindred Konnections. The web site address for the free software is:

http://209.140.72.162/genealogy/download?-1+0+English

There are many useful Internet sites devoted to genealogy. Take a look at some of my favorite genealogy web sites, then start creating your own list of favorites!

As more and more genealogists rely on computers for research, more and more web sites devoted to genealogy will appear. And whether you use e-mail, search engines, software programs, or all of these computer resources, you can be sure that genealogy and computers are a winning combination for bringing the past into the present!

Appendix 1

My Favorite Genealogy Web Sites

Access Genealogy: http://www.accessgenealogy.com/

Ancestry.com: http://www.ancestry.com/

Cyndi's List of Genealogical Web Sites: http://www.CyndisList.com/

Family Tree Maker: http://www.familytreemaker.com/

Genealogy.com: http://www.genealogy.com/

GenForum: http://www.genforum.com/

Kidz GenWeb: http://www.rootsweb.com/~usgwkidz/links.html/

LDS Family Search Website: http://www.familysearch.org/

Mayflower Web Page: http://members.aol.com/calebj/mayflower.html/

U.S. GenWeb Project: http://www.usgenweb.org/

Appendix 2

List of State Abbreviations

Alabama	AL
Alaska	AK
Arizona	AZ
Arkansas	AR
California	CA
Colorado	CO
Connecticut	CT
Delaware	DE
Florida	FL
Georgia	GA
Hawaii	HI
Idaho	ID
Illinois	IL
Indiana	IN
Iowa	IA
Kansas	KS
Kentucky	KY
Louisiana	LA
Maine	ME
Maryland	MD

Massachusetts	MA
Michigan	MI
Minnesota	MN
Mississippi	MS
Missouri	MO
Montana	MT
Nebraska	NE
Nevada	NV
New Hampshire	NH
New Jersey	NJ
New Mexico	NM
New York	NY
North Carolina	NC
North Dakota	ND
Ohio	OH
Oklahoma	OK
Oregon	OR
Pennsylvania	PA
Rhode Island	RI
South Carolina	SC
South Dakota	SD
Tennessee	TN
Texas	TX
Utah	UT
Vermont	VT
Virginia	VA
Washington	WA
West Virginia	WV
Wisconsin	WI
Wyoming	WY

Glossary

Genealogy Dictionary

A Glossary of Genealogical Terms

abt.:

abbreviation for about; used to describe a date in time. (born abt. 1764.)

ancestor:

a person from whom one is descended; forefather.

archives:

a place where public records and historical documents are kept.

aunt:

the sister of one's father or mother.

baptism:

A religious ceremony in which a person is sprinkled with water and admitted into a Christian church.

bef.:

abbreviation for before; used to describe a date in time. (born bef. 1872)

c.:

abbreviation for circa; about. (*"born c. 1600" means born about the year 1600.*)

cemetery:

a place where dead people are buried; graveyard.

census:

an official count of people living in a certain area.

census index:

a book or series of books which contain the names of every person on the census, and where that person is located on the census microfilm.

christening:

to baptize and give a Christian name.

circa:

about; used with dates; abbreviated with the letter "c". (*Born c. 1891; born circa 1891.*)

data:

facts or information.

database:

an organized body of related information.

deceased:

dead

deed:

a legal document written out to show the transfer and/or ownership of a piece of real estate property.

descendant:

a person descended from a particular ancestor.

document:

an official paper that can be used to give proof or information.

forefathers:

a person in your family who lived in an earlier time; ancestor.

genealogist:

a person who studies and researches family histories.

genealogy:

the study of family history.

generation:

all the people in a family who live at the same time; family members of approximately the same age. (*You, your parents, and your grandparents represent three generations of your family.*)

gravestone rubbing:

a paper held up against the flat part of a gravestone, then rubbed with chalk or crayon to reveal data.

kin:

relatives.

maiden name:

a woman's last name before she marries.

marriage:

wedding ceremony

maternal:

relating to the mother's side of a family.

microfiche:

a sheet of film which is able to hold many records, photographs and documents in a small size.

microfilm:

a film which is able to hold many records, photographs and documents in a small size.

obituary:

a notice of someone's death

occupation:

job or profession.

paternal:

relating to the father's side of a family.

pedigree:

a line of ancestors often charted on paper.

sibling:

brother or sister

spouse:

husband or wife.

surname:

a family name; last name.

township:

a portion of a county, similar to a town.

uncle:

the brother of one's mother or father.

widow:

a woman whose husband has died.

widower:

a man whose wife has died.

will:

an official paper that tells what a person wants done with their property after death.

Family Tree Word Search

```
        X K L
      O S G A H S I
    S J A N M G M F R
    K S U R N A M E O Y W
  K E C E L W I L L R S Q O
E Z G T S I G O L A E N E G W
J X A A C R I C U V F M E B X
G N P E E A R Q T I W A H R S S N
P S M C N T P N I H Z N T U G X J F M
X O N S I T F B C B N B H E I R D D X
E W U O L I O R D E S C E N D A N T N
Y S N U I A A Q D A S X R C E M T T N
X V R A T M I O M Y T S G P L P V
  F C G E A Q F B X V R P C L K
W E I M Y R V C I M F Y N W D
  V N S N M E S O O J A A V
      U N N N H W H
        I O I E H
      T T S K G
        S U R
        B O G
        M C X
        O P U
        T D B
        B Q X
```

ancestry	immigration	will
archives	kin	
census	lineage	
circa	maiden name	
cousin	obituary	
descendant	paternal	
forefathers	pedigree	
genealogist	source	
generations	surname	
heir	tombstone	

Genealogy Crossword Puzzle-Easy

ACROSS	DOWN
2. your mother and father	1. your mother's father
4. sister of father or mother	3. always document your _____.
7. abbreviation for "circa"	5. wedding
8. burial place	6. a group of related people
10. keep good records	8. write surnames in _____ letters.
12. brother or sister	9. township

Genealogy Crossword Puzzle-Challenge

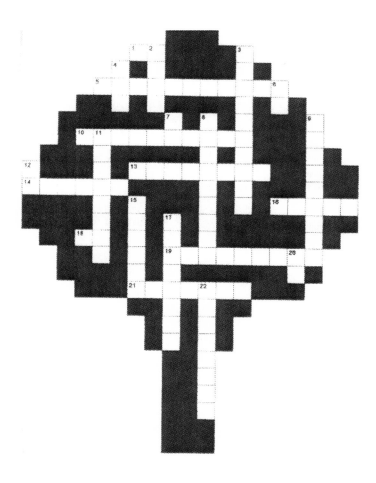

ACROSS	DOWN
1. Maryland (abbrev.)	2. legal land document
5. person who researches family history	3. surname of a woman before marriage
10. job	4. abbreviation for "before"
13. relating to the father	6. Texas (abbrev.)
14. child of an aunt or uncle	7. Pennsylania (abbrev.)
16. about (abbrev. used with dates)	8. a film on which records are kept
18. Virginia (abbrev.)	9. to enter a new country
19. stone erected over a grave	11. war between the states
21. last name	12. South Carolina (abbrev.)
	15. an official count of people
	17. referring to the mother
	20. New York (abbrev.)
	22. place where historical records are kept